The international renowned artist
Thomas Radbruch (born 1945),
photographer of many photo editions and
series, gives his opinion about his
photographs of Lübeck in this city guide:

D0837848

A HEARTY
WELCOME

"It is the crying of the seagulls in the wide
northern sky, the shining bright red of the
brick stones, the copper green of the spires
and the peaks of the towers, the golden,
gleaming, ancient, cobbled surface of the
streets in the afternoon sun.

Light and shadow play in the narrow
alley-ways and courtyards and create
magic corners and nooks.

Like the masts of a big sailing ship,
heading into the sky in cool and clear lines,
the towers of the churches are towering
above everything, reflecting in the water
at the same time.
Loaded richly with treasures like Venice,
its southern relative, Lübeck is sailing through
the time of megabits and microchips."

Yours

Thomas Radbruch

In the 15th Century LUBICE, "the Lovely", was the third biggest town of the Holy Roman Empire of the German Nation and **"Queen of the Hanse League"**. There are two characteristic features that influence the outward appearance of the town and the way the citizens of Lübeck see

Panorama of the town hill from a wood-engraving of 1552

themselves: on one hand the trade and on the other hand the status of a free town of the Holy Roman Empire.

Lübeck would not be the same without trade and the harbour. The route of the salt goes via Lübeck towards Scandinavia. The Hanseatic League was founded to protect the transport routes. And with its expansion the **power and the richness** of Lübeck increased. Hanseatic merchants had integrity and they were cosmopolitan. If there was money to earn in a trade, origins were of no importance.

In the protestant tradition work and life can not be regarded separately. The sales office (Kontor) was situated on the ground floor of the merchants' big houses; the storage room was in the cellar and the family lived in well furnished surroundings in the 1st floor, the belétage. The carts loaded with goods drove directly through the big entrance doors on the ground floor and through the portal.

Seal of the Town of Lübeck from 1255 with a sailor and a merchant in a ship

Since the German Emperor Friedrich II. Barbarossa confirmed the rights of Lübeck in the Freedom from Empire Contract (Reichsfreiheitsbrief) of 1226, Lübeck was a free town of the Holy Roman Empire and was only subjugated by the Roman-German emperor, but apart from this

1143 first German foundation of a town on the Baltic Ocean

1157 destruction caused by a fire of the town

1159 new foundation by Henry the Lion

they had sole responsibility. With the expansion of the Hanseatic League along the Baltic Ocean Region the dispensation of the justice of Lübeck set standards.

The town being not subjugated to any feudalistic lord, the citizens and the merchants of Lübeck adopted the function of aristocrats, however, without giving up their social responsibility. They donated institutions for poor and ill people – thereby erecting a memorial statue for themselves. Even nowadays the entrepreneurs of Lübeck follow this tradition and are financially and ideally engaged in the town.

The closed townscape of medieval brickstone buildings is the reason for Lübeck's attractiveness of today and its place on the **UNESCO** list as **World Heritage Site of Mankind**. Many visitors enjoy the idyll of the ancient part of the town, its cosy alley-ways, the contemplative atmosphere in the sacral buildings and the submerging into a former time. A time when exactly these medieval brickstone buildings had been an expression of richness, power, independence, fortification, claim to leadership and social responsibility.

1161 seat of the bishop, origin of the brick stone gothic architecture

1226 Free town (of the Holy Roman Empire)

1241 Hansestadt

1293 to 1669 Queen of the Hanse League medieval economic power

1866 Joining of the North German Union

1871 independent Federal State

1911 Lübeck becomes a bigger city

1942 Target of the allied bombs in the Second World War

after 1945 Arrival of refugees from the Eastern European Regions

1964 University City

1987 UNESCO World Heritage Site

TOUR THROUGH THE
ANCIENT PART OF LÜBECK

PUPPENBRÜCKE

Free translation:

In Lübeck on the Puppenbrücke
stands Mercury, the god.

He's quite a well-built sort of guy.
Much clothing he wears not.

Far away in his Roman heaven
he never learned 'bout shirts.

So strangers might admire his
bare bottom from backwards.

Emanuel Geibel

INSIDER-TIP

Surely you will realize at the end of your tour, that
you enjoyed it, and that you would like to come back.
Then go back to the Puppenbrücke and touch coura-
geously the naked backside of the messenger of the
Gods. This lucky grip will lead you back to the Hanseatic Town of Lübeck.

The quickest way to start the tour to the island of the old
town center is from the Art Nouveau main station along
the **Puppenbrücke ❶** in the direction of the Holstentor.
"Puppets" is the affectionate short word for the **8 Roman
Gods** originating from the 18th century.

Apart from Mercury, the Trade protection God, the following figures form a line on the right and left side of the
bridge: the river God of the Trave, the Concord, the Peace,
the Intelligence, a Roman
Warrior symbolizing the
virtues of the citizens, the
Freedom and Neptun for
the Baltic Ocean.

The present figures are reconstructed of artificial stone.
You can find the originals
made of sandstone in the **St. Annen Museum**.
After detecting that the exhaust fumes cause irreparable
damage to the sandstone figures, they were replaced.

As soon as you have crossed the **Puppenbrücke**, you reach the famous **landmark** of Lübeck: identification object of the citizens and main attraction point of the town.

The **Holstentor** **2** originated in the year 1478, even if the inscription of the throughway says something different. Its function as the south west town gate can be recognized by comparing both parts of the building.

There is an impenetrable bulwark on the outside of the town, in which you can see small **embrasures** hinting at the fortification of the town. On the other side, facing the town, there are small window openings softening the front, as there was no danger, against which one should have weaponed, coming from the inner part of the town.

Opening hours
April – Sept.
10.00 am to 5.00 pm.
Oct. – March
10.00 am to 4.00 pm
closed on Mondays

In former times the Holstentor was a landmark of the liberty of Lübeck as a town, today the building is a museum of the History of Lübeck and the History of Seafaring.

Originally both towers were fitted with open fireplaces, leading to the chimneys beside the dormers.

A cross-section drawing through the south tower of the Holstentor preparing to defend, drawn by Mr. Pieper, construction director.

48 fire guns fully armed and with the use of all gun embrasures defended the town against attackers from outside – cannonballs were fired from downstairs, hand guns were fired steeply downwards from the upper floors.

At the time when the Holstentor was constructed from 1460 on, the countryside belonging to Holstein in front of the Holstentor was under the command of the territorial power of Denmark.

Even when the fame of Lübeck began to decrease, at that moment the free town of Lübeck, which was only subjugated by the Roman German Emperor, wanted to defend themselves from the Danish in front of the gates of Lübeck.

INSIDER-TIP

Visit the museum inside the Holstentor and get to know more about the history of Lübeck and the history of seafaring of the "Queen of the Hanse League".
The torture instruments in the cellar vault of the Holstentor makes visitors shiver when they imagine the use during the medieval times.

The architect Hinrich Helmstede did not only build a **defensive work** for the town, but at the same time a memorial of the hanseatic self-confidence and urban claim of power.

In 1863 the demolition of the building could be prevented only by a hair's breadth – with a majority of exactly one vote. Instead of this, extensive restoration works started, which were finished in 1871, the year of the foundation of the empire, and which show the Holstentor slightly changed but in its complete beauty.

The inscription CONCOR-DIA DOMI FORIS PAX points out to every person entering the town, "to keep concord inside the house and peace outside".

On the other side of the river Trave the living house of the Stecknitz-sailors, who carried the salt to Lübeck with their small boats, was directly situated on the river.

The former **salt lofts** ❸ of the town stand close together just beside the Holstentor. The six brick stone **gabled houses** were built between 1579 and 1745. Originally they were used as a storage room for salten herrings, which were very much desired as a fasting food and which were imported from Skåne (Southern Sweden). Afterwards the salt lofts were important for the more lucrative trade with salt. The **"white gold"** was transported by small boats along the Stecknitz channel or on carts along the country roads from the salines of Lüneburg.

The federal road from Lübeck to Lüneburg even now carries the name **"old salt road"**. The salt was shipped from Lübeck to Scandinavia, into the Baltic countries and to Russia, where it was used to salt fish.

The **cogs** returned with furs, train oil or ore and guaranteed the richness of the merchants of the town.

During the times of the National Socialist Regime the salt lofts were used as meeting rooms for the Hitler Youth. Today there is a traditional **clothing store** inside the building.

INSIDER-TIP

Open pleasure boats leave from across the bridge, between Holstentor, salt lofts and town center, for a tour around the old town island. In brilliant sunshine you can enjoy the marvellous view of the fronts of the houses from the water and you get to know a lot of new and interesting things.

Symbols of Lübeck's prosperity in brickstone: in the foreground the salt lofts in which the salt was stored; behind St. Marienkirche, the church of the merchants, dealing with the "white gold."

You should not use the direct way along the Holsten-straße to the market place, but turn left. After having passed the Holstentor and the Salt Lofts, turn to the street "An der Untertrave". Now enjoy strolling along the **harbour of ancient ships. 4**

Brickstone fronts of the old storage houses and St. Marienkirche in the background.

Pure nostalgia

Uncountable old **ancient ships and traditional sailing boats**, restorated and kept in good condition with a lot of love and even more means, are presented along the quai.

The "Fridtjof Nansen" accompanied the Norwegian explorer to the North Pole as a provisions boat.

In medieval times the **cogs** were moored here. Along the Untertrave you will find a lot of wonderful old storage houses, in which the loads of the cogs were stored.

Situated at the edge of
the roof of the MUK
(Music and Congress Hall)
the figure ensemble called
"the strangers" of
Thomas Schütte reminds of
the destiny of more than
100.000 refugees from the
East, finding a home in
Lübeck after 1945.

Turn to one of the side streets, preferrably the **Mengstraße**, and you will go "uphill" into the direction of the town hall and the St. Marienkirche.

To your right and to your left a lot of houses with **historical fronts** can be discovered. You will find the oldest German wine import house, established 1678, in the **Tesdorpf-Haus** at the corner Mengstraße/An der Unter- **TIP** trave. Get advice for the choice of an original Lübecker Rotspon and enjoy the historical premises.

In the restaurant **Schabbelhaus** (Mengstr. 48-50) the ✗ interieur gives an impression of the upper class lifestyle of the hanseatic merchants, which you should enjoy a little bit more while drinking good wine.

The circular "holes" in the wall of the town hall are of the year 1434. They minimize the pressure of the wind blowing against the wall and protect it from collapsing.

The renaissance stairs of 1594 guiding to the war room of the town hall.

The town hall, as a unity of different style epoques, forms the border of the **Kohlmarkt** 5 at its north eastern side.

Guided tours in the town hall Mo-Fr at 11.00 am, 12.00 am and 3.00 pm.
Changes due to unforeseen circumstances.

Through the arcades of the **"Langes Haus"** you enter the pedestrian precinct of the Breite Straße. In former times goldsmiths presented their goods under the gothic pointed archs. You can see the parent company of **Niederegger**, which made the **Lübecker Marzipan** famous all over the world, from the Breite Straße just directly opposite of the **Renaissance stairs** of the town hall (1594). Even if the people of Lübeck did not invent this "confectionery of the harem" and even if it supposedly came over from Venice to Lübeck, the bakers produce the "marci panis", meaning the bread of the Markus, since more than 500 years.

INSIDER-TIP

In the "marzipan salon" (2nd floor) of the parent company Niederegger you get to know more about the history of marzipan and you will discover many possible variances of the sugar-almond-pastry.

On your way back stop at the café Niederegger (1st floor) and taste the legendary Lübecker nut cake.

(Nearly) everything belonging to a typical visit of Lübeck: north German shower of rain, puddles on the cobblestones and brick stone wherever you look!

The highest point of the island of the old town center is decorated by the "Grande Dame" among all the churches in the old town center. The "Church of the Council" unites innumerable superlatives in its walls. The construction of the Marienkirche was started in 1250 and was accomplished in 1350. **The Marienkirche** **6** is the third biggest church in Germany.

The construction was architecturally copied from examples in France and Flanders – and for the first time it was tried to copy the language of the forms of the **high gothic** from hard natural stone into rough brick stone. The nave measures about 38,3 m and you can look up to the world's highest brick stone vault. In the southern part of the building you can see the world's biggest mechanical organ.

Opening hours
April – September
10:00 am – 6.00 pm
October – March
10:00 am – 4:00/5:00 pm
depending on the daylight

The quarter of the merchants extended between the lofts at the shore of the river Trave up to the Marienkirche.

Right side:
The narrow proportions inside the cathedral force the view of the spectator up into the sky.

A large part of the town center as well as St. Petrikirche and St. Marienkirche burned completely down after the bomb attack in the **Palmarum Night** from 28th March to 29th March 1942.

The **bells** in the South Tower are witness to this event. In the night of the falling bombs the bells fell down from the burning roof truss and buried themselves into the floor.

With the complete restoration of the church the ruins of the bells were left in their place in memory of all dead people far from their home countries.

Contemporary witnesses of the night of the bombs remember the sound of the bells above the burning church before the roof and the peak of the church collapsed.

Left side:

One of the jewels of the history of art and religious art in St. Marienkirche: the astronomical clock. At noon the running of the figures is set into motion and you can hear the bell ringing.

INSIDER-TIP

None of the churches in the town center are so rich of legends as St. Marienkirche.

The legend of the mouse and the rose bush was immortalized in the form of a small stone mouse in St. Marienkirche. Look for it and touch the animal with your left hand... this will bring you good luck!

Sculpture of a little devil
next to the portal of St. Marien
created by Rolf Goerler.

View from the high choir to the biggest mechanical organ in the world with 8.512 pipes.

The most famous organist of the Marienkirche was Dietrich Buxtehude.

Even Johann Sebastian Bach travelled to Lübeck to hear him play.

Right side:

The vaults of St. Marien: created as an image of the firmament on earth and inspired by the believe that God is the light. Gothic architecture is never arbitrary. The colors of the interior, architectural dimensions, the number of the columns and the number of cross vaults were carefully chosen and show the religious relationship of the medieval picture and form language.

During the restoration of the holy fresks left from around 1300 the Lübeck artist Lothar Malskat completed some motives from his own draft and caused the greatest scandal of art forgery in the young Federal Republic of Germany.

If you want to know more about the uncomparable architecture of St. Marien-kirche, we recommend to you a **guided tour into the tower and the vault**.
The way leads up narrow tower stairs, along the ceiling of the vault up to the carillon in the **bell cage**. That is the way to get to know St. Marienkirche of an undreamt height. The **guided tours in the evening** are the most impressive ones.

For the guided tour lasting about two hours we recommend walking shoes, we do not recommend this tour to those who have fear of heights and claustrophobia.

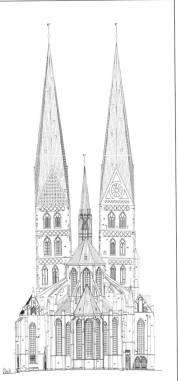

Guided tours
into the tower and the vault
from April to September
Saturdays 3:15 pm,
during the summer months
on Wednesdays 3:15 pm,
in June every evening
additionally.

A marvellous view of the ancient part of the town compensates for the strenous clambering onto the roof through the narrow stairs of the tower.

View through the arcades cloister at the back of the town hall.

Praying in the mayor chapel was the councilors' duty before a council meeting.

Going down the pedestrian area, just directly between St. Marienkirche and the **building of the chancellery**, there is a romantic path of **7** **arcades** up to the doors of the **Buddenbrookhaus** in Mengstraße 4. From 1484 onwards the building of the chancellery served as a writing room of the council and was piece by piece expanded and extended.

Even if it was not Thomas and Heinrich Mann's birthplace, both of them had spent a meaningful time during their childhood in this house.

The **Buddenbrookhaus**  belonged to their grandfather and – with its big gothic cellar vaults – served the famous literates' father as financial office and as storage room.

Opening hours:
Up to 31st March
Monday – Sunday
10:00 am to 5:00 pm
from 1st April onwards:
Monday to Sunday
10:00 am to 6:00 pm

Information telephone:
0451-122 41 92
www.buddenbrookhaus.de

Already in the first chapter of the "Budden-brooks" the building is described in detail.

Since the new opening of the **"Heinrich-and-Thomas-Mann-Center"** in June 2000, fixed exhibitions give information about the novel, its author and his family. On the ground floor you visit "The Manns – the writer's family" and in the second floor you get to know more about "The Buddenbrooks – a century novel". The rooms in the belétage were reconstructed along Thomas Mann's descriptions in his novel "The Buddenbrooks". They do not show the domestic life of the family Mann, but literature.

A "walkable novel": Pathway from the "room of the goods" into the "landscape room" with baptism cup and family bible of the Mann family.

In the novel published in 1901 similarity to real people did not exist by pure chance, but definitely intentional. This fact was an enormous offence for those dignitaries of Lübeck who recognized themselves under different names as characters in the novel. The **Nobel Prize of Literature** was given to Thomas Mann in 1929, but the bourgeoisie of Lübeck, finding their "hanseatic attitude of mind" now immortalized in the world literature, could only be partly reconciled.

Named after the publisher
and "discoverer" of
Thomas Mann,
the Samuel-Fischer-Library
contains – behind a thick
oak boarding – an extensive
collection of the family Mann,
which is made available for
scientific research.

The "room of the Gods":

Parts of the interieur stay
veiled, so that the reader
need not completely say
goodbye to his imagined
rooms.

Further down the pedestrian precinct into the Breite Straße, keep in the direction **St. Jacobi**, the church of the sailors and seafarers. Just opposite it the **Schiffergesellschaft** **9** invites you, being the "most classical pub in the world". Founded in 1535 as a room for authorities and meetings of the fraternity of sailors and seafarers, the original rooms are nowadays used as a **restaurant**.

The God's cellar beneath the Schiffergesellschaft is recommended for a good sip in Christian seafarer-atmosphere.

The **Nikolaus-Fraternity** was founded in 1401 and in the beginning was a communion of destitutes. During the following time it worked particularly hard for social concerns. Every "setting out to sea" in former times meant the risk of never coming back from this journey.

The surviving dependants, widows and orphans were supported as well as other needy people.

Even nowadays you can become a member of the **Shipper's guild**, if you have got a license for high seas, command or commanded a sea-going vessel and live in the near surroundings of Lübeck.

In the Schiffergesellschaft take your seat on real planks of a ship, the so called "blowouts". Before you are full up with the rich interior decor, you should preferably taste a typical seafarer dish like "Labskaus". This dish gives you an impression of how limited food and lifestyle aboard were in former times.

Engelsgrube – its name does not refer to the winged creatures of heaven (Engel = angel), as one might think according to the surroundings of St. Jacobikirche, but to the Englishmen who – in times of the Hanseatic League – were allowed to use this part of the harbour to load and unload their ships.

If you do not turn towards St. Jacobi, but in the direction of the shore of the river Trave, then you follow down the **Engelsgrube**. **10** To your right and to your left you find on both sides of the streets innumerable **residential alleyways**, in which, in former times, the box carriers and the salt packers lived.

Real alley-ways-atmosphere:

During the summer people play in the traffic-calmed alley-ways and walks.

Right side:

View into the Fischergrube:

Alleys and streets in the old town center still carry nowadays the name of the occupational group that lived and worked there.

At house number 43 the Bäckergang (walk of the bakers) joins two alley-ways, it is the only one in Lübeck.

Even though the lovingly restored **accomodations in the alley-ways** have the charm of an open air exhibition, they are however vivid living areas full of daily life.

As a lover of highbrow sacral music, you should inform yourself about the concert events in St. Jacobi. The smaller Stellwagen organ from the 16th century and the bigger one of the year 1504 made St. Jacobi famous for its organ concerts.

St. Jacobi, **⓫** the church of sailors and seafarers, was mentioned for the first time in 1227. Contrary to St. Marien and St. Petri, the church survived the bomb attack in 1942 without any damage, so that the art treasures like the **Brömse-Altar** of the 15th century and the uncovered **wall paintings** with the pictures of apostles and saints of the 14th century have been maintained until today.

During medieval times St. Jacobi was a fixed place for Scandinavian pilgrims on their way to Santiago de Compostela, Spain.

Today the sister ship of the "Pamir", the "Passat", lies fixed at anchor in Travemünde.

A document of the recent seafarer history is found in the north tower chapel. The last **life boat of the "Pamir"** reminds you of the sinking of the sailing school ship in 1957. When it sank in a hurricane in the Atlantic Ocean only 6 of the 86 men crew of the four-master were rescued. Today the rescued life boat is a memorial for all seafaring men who have died in the ocean.

A view in the bell tower of St. Jacobi.

Right side:
Many sailors lived in the quarter of Maria-Magdalena, named after the present Burgkloster. It is situated between Engelsgrube, St. Jacobi and the Burgtor.

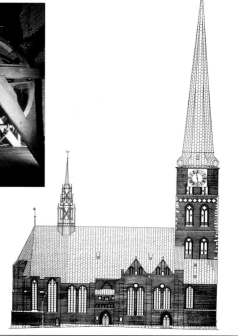

A view normally reserved only for the pidgeons:
view over the Breite Straße to St. Marien.

As soon as you enter the **Große Burgstraße** you can see the **Burgtor** 🔢 towering up at the end of the street. It was documented in 1224 for the first time. Four storeys were added to the tower in 1444. The originally steaply pointed roof was set on fire in 1685, and it then was changed, according to the fashion of that time, into a baroque bonnet, which in contrary to many copper roofs of the town is not covered with the green patina of the verdigris. To the right and to the left of the Burgtor you find the remainders of the medieval **town wall**.

Left side:

The alternating use of glazed and unglazed brickstones creates the red-black winding shape of the Burgtor.

If you want to discover the old town island coming from the North through the Burgtor, you are in very noble company.
Even in 1806 **Marshall Bernadotte** fell into the town in this way while it was defended by Blücher. The Prussian general did not "go up" to it, as the proverb will have us believe, but instead scarpered with his troops, until he was confronted in Ratekau. And nowadays the **"Blüchereiche"** over there reminds us of this event.

INSIDER-TIP

Go on a guided tour in one of the roofless buses from the LVG from Lübeck to Travemünde and try to find a seat in the first row of the upper deck (departure at Untertrave). For a second your breath will stop while the bus driver guides his monster of a bus in a virtuoso manner through the archway of the Burgtor.

On the left side of the Burgtor the horses and the fleet of vehicles were stored in the "Marstall".

Opening hours
April - September
10:00 am to 5:00 pm
October – March
10:00 am – 4:00 pm
Closed on Mondays
1st Thursday in the month
opened till 9:00 pm

Coming from the town center along a peak-arched castle way, on your left side in front of the Burgtor you reach the **culture forum Burgkloster**. **13** This most important of all medieval **monastery plants** in North Germany was founded in 1229 A.D. as the Maria-Magdalenen-Kloster.

On the Saint's Day of the Saint Maria-Magdalena, the 21st of July, German Princes in the battle of Bornhöved conquered the Danish troops and with this they ended the Danish dominance in the Baltic region.

Roofscape of Burgtor and
Große Burgstraße

As a sign of their gratitude that God gave this victory to them, the people of Lübeck erected a **Dominikanerkloster** inside the town walls on the land which was claimed by the Danish until then. In the course of history the monastery was used as a home for poor people, a court and a remand prison. The ancient walls experienced their darkest moment when in the year 1943 the "Christians' court case" ended with the death of four clergymen who resisted the national-socialistic regime bravely from the pulpit.

INSIDER-TIP
In the impressive cellar vaults of the Burgkloster you find the "treasure of the Hanse merchant" as a permanent exhibition. In 1984, during soil construction work, a wooden box was found containing innumerable European gold and silver coins. This valuable find turned out to be the "exchange cash" of a merchant of Lübeck and documented the world wide trade relations of the Hanseatic town.

Since its restoration by the federal state of Schleswig-Holstein, the **culture forum** Burgkloster serves as a culture center for the town of Lübeck. Changing events about art, architecture, the history of the Hanse League and the Baltic region, philosophy and contemporary history, but also music, plays and readings found their place here.

The night of the museum which takes place every year in September, provides special events, longer opening hours and a reduced entrance fee for families for all cultural places of Lübeck. It offers no chance for culture grouches to find an excuse to stay on the sofa.

Architectural convertion of silence and prayer: medieval monastery construction art in its pure format is seen in the refectory of the Burgkloster.

Warehouse no. 6 attracts visitors with live music. From the Burgkloster narrow alley-ways and stairs lead down to the **Burgtorhafen**. ⑭ The old storage houses at the quai were reconstructed in the Nineties and are nowadays venues with a cosy and rustic atmosphere.

Going down the Untertrave into the direction of the Holstentor you find one of the oldest storage houses in the town.

Once owned by the Mann family, today an auction house is established under the low ceilings of this storage house.

"Die Eiche" (An der Unter-trave 34) is a hidden secret for those loving antic art and junk.

Opening hours
April - September
10:00 am to 5:00 pm
October – March
10:00 am – 4:00 pm
Closed on Mondays

Chimes at 9:55 am,
11:55 am, 3:55 pm and
at 5:55 pm

The **Heiligen-Geist-Hospital** as well as St. Jacobi boarders the Koberg.

In former times, donated by the merchants of Lübeck as a welfare institution for old and ill people, it was not only one of the **oldest social institutions of Germany**, but at the same time one of the most important monumental buildings of the medieval age.

Parallel to St. Jacobi and with a wonderful view to the Koberg you find the "Pastorenhäuser" (Preachers' houses) of 1604. Since their extravagant restoration they are used for municipality purposes.

You enter the oldest part of the building by the green entry portal. The jewels of the church are the **paintings of the Lettner balustrade**. The legend of Elisabeth is presented on 23 oak wooden tables. Originating from the 14th century, they belong to the most important medieval **wall paintings** of the town.

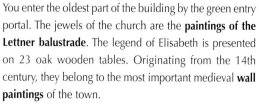

The huge cellar vaults were formerly used as storage rooms and deposit of goods. Since 1955 a wine pub is situated in here, which was expanded to a restaurant in the course of time. Around the Koberg a lot of **restaurants, bistros and cafés** invite you to sit "comfortably outside"!

View over the turret of the
Heiligen-Geist-Hospital,
corresponding to the style
of the 17th century.

Up to the seventies old
people and people in need
of care lived in wooden
chambers of 4 to 6 m^2
called "Kabäuschen" in
German.

The Gods' statues on the Behnhaus incorporate important attributes and characteristics which a successful merchant should have. So you find, among others, cautiousness, luck and hope.

Follow the **Königstraße** **16** further up, and discover the houses no. 9 and no. 11 as two of the most beautiful classical buildings of the town.

Behnhaus

With its big and representative interior hall construction and its upper balustrade crowned with the Gods' pictures, it is one of the last town houses in a grand style.

The „Blue Room" in the Behnhaus.

Museum Drägerhaus –
Flügelsaal.

Already in 1920 art friends of Lübeck bought the building
and gave it to the town as a **museum**.

Since its opening in 1923 the Behnhaus is a museum for
paintings, craft work and sculptures of the 19th and 20th
century. Next to the works of Edvard Munch, you find
protagonists of the German
impressionism, as Lieber-
mann, Slevogt and Corinth.
Representatives of the 19th
century are Friedrich Over-
beck of Lübeck and Caspar
David Friedrich.

INSIDER-TIP

Heads up! And this should be taken literally.
The beauty of the fronts of some houses in the town
center is only seen from the higher floors
(see Behnhaus Statues).

In the garden of the Behnhaus the Overbeck-Gesellschaft,
an association of art lovers, show international art from
the classical modern area up to present times in their
pavillon.

Drägerhaus

Thanks to a **foundation of Dr. Heinrich Dräger**, an indus-
trialist and patron of the town of Lübeck, house no. 9 was
bought and restored. On the ground floor of the garden
wing you find the only, but completely preserved banquet
hall sequence of the 18th century in Lübeck.
On the first floor you can see the intérieur of the Bieder-
meier era and crafts work of modern times.

Opening hours
Behnhaus and Drägerhaus
April - September
10:00 am to 5:00 pm
October – March
10:00 am – 4:00 pm
Closed on Mondays
1st Thursday in the month
opened till 9:00 pm

Opening hours
April - September
10:00 am to 1:00 pm and
2:00 pm to 5:00 pm
Closed on Mondays

St. Katharinen **17** is the only preserved **monastery church** in Lübeck. It was the heart of the Franciscan Order in the complete Baltic area. In contrary to the other five churches in the town center, which constructed the silhouette of Lübeck with the seven tower peaks, St. Katharinen has **no tower**. The rules of the order of the Franciscans did not allow this luxury. And thanks to the **plague epidemics** haunting Lübeck, St. Katharinen got its size and expansion. Due to generous donations, this new basilique was constructed on the heritage of its romanesque predecessor.

INSIDER-TIP

If you want to fill your little squirts with enthusiasm then you should look at the stones of the slim limestone columns in the cross vault with them. They all show depictions of the fable "Reinecke fox".

The three figures of **Ernst Barlach** "woman in the wind", "beggar" and "singing monastery pupil" (see picture below) are only the first three figures of twelve which make up the cycle called "community of the Saints".

Between 1930 and 1932 Barlach´s trio came into being, but then the nazis censored his art for being "degenerated". The work remained unfinished and the figures hidden in the cellar vaults.

Katharina von Alexandria, by legend a beautiful and extremely intelligent woman, gave her name to the church. She was tortured for defending her faith, bound to a wheel and found the death of a martyrer.

During the restoration in 1949 the sculptor Gerhard Marcks of Lübeck completed the figures' frieze.

Since 1805 St. Katharinen has been profanized and used as a museum , you find an "art highlight" in between the walls of the church. You can admire "The Awakening of the Lazarus", by **Jacopo Tintoretto** of the year 1578, being enlightened after throwing in a coin.

At nearly the same time as Günter Grass was awarded the 1999 Nobel Prize of Literature, the **Günter Grass-Haus** (18) was opened in 2002 as a "forum for literature and graphic art" in the **Glockengießerstraße 21**.

Opening hours:
Up to 31st March
Monday – Sunday
10:00 am to 5:00 pm
from 1st April onwards:
Monday to Sunday
10:00 am to 6:00 pm

As the author of the Danzig Trilogy, consisting of the "Tin Drum", "Cat and Mouse", and "Dog Years", Grass has achieved worldwide fame. His oeuvre as an artist, a studied sculptor and a graphics is not so well known. This is changed by an exhibition of his plastics in the **sculptor garden**.

The Grass collection consists of a total stock of graphic reproductive works, documents of his literary work after 1995, a specialist library and an archive. As a place of exhibitions and research of the multiple talents of an artist, the Günter Grass-Haus is also a forum for **permanently changing events** on this subject.

Information telephone:
0451-122 41 92
www.guenter-grass-haus.de

The Kunsthaus in Lübeck represents the graphical and sculptural work of Günter Grass as well as the pictural work of Armin Müller-Stahl and is situated only a few meters away from the Günter Grass-Haus, in the Königstr. 20.

Sculpture "Butt im Griff" in the atrium of the Günter Grass-Haus – donated by Erika and Frank-Thomas Gaulin.

Along the outer wall of St. Katharinen you find your way down the **Glockengießerstraße**. **19** Even if it is not a sign of good education to look into other peoples' windows, you should pay attention of the courts and alley-ways along the street.

INSIDER-TIP

Next to the Günter Grass-Haus in the Glockengießerstraße you find the photo atelier of Thomas Radbruch. During the opening hours Tuesday – Sunday from 11:00 am to 6:00 pm you find all of his photographs, books and arts postcards there.

On request, there is the possibility of having a very personal souvenir. For appointments: 0451/707 03 91 and 0171/216 38 15.

In the old town center, the so called **"Wohnstifte – "court-yards of the charities"** have a long tradition, and can be traced back to the medieval time. Prosperous citizens of the town showed their social responsibilities in donating charity foundations, maybe also with the hope of coming a little bit closer to their desired place in paradise. A lot of institutions for old and poor people were constructed as well as for widows and orphans of sailors and merchants.

Füchtingshof, Glockengießerstraße 23-27, with 21 original

Row of houses along the Glockengießerstraße with St. Katharinen in the background.

appartments is the biggest and most beautiful **Stiftungshof**. The merchant and councillor Johann Füchting gave one third of his estate "for the use and for the best of the poor people" and with this financed the construction of the accomodation.

Glandorps Hof and Illhornstift, Glockengießerstraße 39-53. Glandorps Hof is the oldest among the courtyards of the charities, and its construction was financed by the councillor and merchant Johann Glandorp.

Adjoining this is Glandorps Gang, where poor widows of merchants and craftsmen lived in cabins of about 16m^2 in former times. An extensive redevelopment of the complete complex was finished in 1977.

Behind the medieval facade there are modern living units for senior citizens, handicapped people and families with many children today. The original purpose of the donation was transferred into modern times.

Füchtingshof in the Glockengießerstraße. At its end, in the first floor, the head's room rises above the court among the block of houses.

From this position the head of the old people's home had a good view of the situation in the court and took care for law and order.

The Füchtingshof is daily opened and can be visited from 9:00 am to 12:00 am and from 3:00 pm to 5:00 pm. While entering the court, please show consideration regarding the inhabitants of the court.

Romantic alley-ways and luxurious shops.

If you have followed this guide trustfully, you are now situated in the Glockengießerstraße. From here a lot of ways lead to our next stop, the St. Aegidien-Kirche.

Maybe you are more of the **shopping type**? Then we recommend the way back through the Königstraße. ●

INSIDER-TIP

Even if you do not expect it here, in the Glocken-gießerstraße there are some very special shops with romantic court yards and a lot of Lübeck flair.

Here you find extraordinary florists as well as exotic colourful living accessories, exclusive jewellery design up to outstanding robe clothing, dressmaking and tailoring – take your time and just "look in"!

On this road you find the Löwen Apotheke (Lion's pharmacy) (the oldest gothic citizens' house in Lübeck), the **König-Passage** – for long-lasting shopping tours in a short distance – **ice cream parlours, fashion boutiques, cafés, department stores and shoe shops**.

You will find everything you want in the **Fleischhauer-, Hüx- and Wahmstraße**.

Especially the **Hüxstraße** offers individual **shopping flair** – beside delicious food, designer fashion, modern art, jewellery or coffee and tea specialities as well as garments, art, antique dealers, books and exclusive interior.

For the refreshment of your spirits some recommendable **restaurants and cafés** with their gardens and terraces in the atrium invite you to sit outside. The former coachhouse of the **"Alte Rösterei"** (Wahmstraße 43-45) lodges today – instead of carts, coaches and horses – a charming bistro with possibilities to sit outside.

Perhaps you could not get enough of the narrow alley-ways, **20** crooked houses, medieval fronts and cobble stones?

Then you should go down the Glockengießerstraße and turn to your right. Through the alleys Tünkenhagen, Rosengarten, Bei St. Johannis, Schlumacherstraße, Balauerfohr and St. Annen-Straße you go straight ahead towards St. Aegidien-Kirche.

Opening hours
Tuesday – Saturday
10:30 am to 12.00 am
and 3:00 pm - 4:00 pm
October – March
2:00 pm to 3:00 pm

Opposite the church in
the Aegidienhof there is
the Marli-Café and restaurant open all day long.
Large-scaled windows
offer a marvellous view
over the shadowy court
yard. The café is run by
the Marli – Werkstätten, a
charitable institution for
handicapped people.

"Small, but fine" is the slogan for **St. Aegidien**. **21**
The church is the smallest among all the churches of the
town center of Lübeck, a three-roomed hall construction
with an elevated platform in the middle.

Traditionally it is the church of the craftsmen and treasu-
rers, who lived and worked in this part of the town. Inside the church gothic **wall-paintings** were uncovered
under the white-washed walls. Archeologists and histori-
ans hold the opinion, that during the medieval age, the
whole church was painted in this way. Since 1921, at
Christmas time a Low German nativity play is performed.
In the summer, the shadowy **court yard** of St. Aegidien
invites you for a rest.

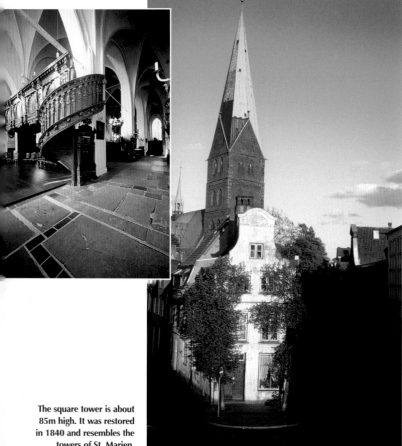

The square tower is about
85m high. It was restored
in 1840 and resembles the
towers of St. Marien.

In the spring of 2003 the arts hall St. Annen opened its doors.

Art, photography and sculptures are shown beside permanently changing exhibitions.

Constructed as a monastery building for the order of the Augustines in 1502, the monastery closed in 1532, due to the reformation coming to North Germany sooner than expected. Since then, **St. Annen 22** served many functions; in 1915 a **museum** was erected inside its walls, which emphasizes the sacral art of the medieval age.

The gothic building, in which you find, among others, a cloister, a refectory, and a chapter, each room close to each other, has got the biggest collection of completely preserved **carving altars** in Germany. All exhibits have their origin in Lübeck and give a reference to the prosperity of the Hanseatic town in the medieval age.

Close to the St. Annen Museum, there is the Jewish parish synagoge in Lübeck.

Inaugurated in 1880 as a domed construction in an oriental-arabesque style, it was plundered and set on fire during the pogrom night of the 9th November 1938.

In 1945 it was given back to the Jewish parishoners and was restored.

The collection of the altars in the gothic ambience in St. Annen is, all together, an impressive collective artwork. In the upper floors, which were added later on, the visitors get an impression of the **citizens' of Lübeck way of life**. Furniture, porcelain, faiences, silver and toys from the medieval age up to the 19th century can be seen. Complete rooms are designed according to the style of singular epoques, from the furniture up to the silk wall coverings from Italy.

The towers of the cathedral and a part of the storage house. Despite frequent changes to the construction plans, the expansion of the romanesque basilique to a gothic hall church amounts to a harmonic whole.

At the roads leading up to the junction of **St.-Annen-Straße/Mühlenstraße 23** you should follow absolutely your heart! If you dream of fried potatoes, Quiche Lorraine, spaghetti carbonara or chili con carne, or only of coffee with a muffin or a bagel, you had better turn to your left immediately. ⬤

Culinary delights

Along the Mühlenstraße in the direction of the Mühlenbrücke there is a great variety of **restaurants and cafés** and a decision where to go is not easily made:

Facades of the "Musterbahn" with a view to the left on the pub "Alter Zolln".

Before joining the military service, the recruits were "given their medical" here for their military service fitness.

The "Alte Zolln", a former custom house and now one of the oldest pubs in Lübeck, is captivating by its rustic atmosphere.

In traditional pubs you find small snacks as well as solid home cooking. During the summer months restaurants and bistros with their contemplative beer gardens at the Krähenteich tempt you to **"sit outside and watch people going by"**.

Whether you make up your mind for French bistro flair, a fashionable in-crowd bar, a texmex bar or the classical Italian restaurant, it's a question of your own taste. The small Milbridge coffee shop offers an inexhaustible selection to the demanding experts of the roasted beans – also for take away.

Beside the Holstentor and the Burgtor, there were two other gates belonging to the town fortification: The **Mühlentor** and the **Hüxtertor**. There are no remains left.

DOM

You walk down the St. Annen Straße up to the end and cross the Mühlenstraße, your way goes through the "Fegefeuer" (purgatory) into the "Paradies" (paradise).

The **"Fegefeuer"**, a turning from the Mühlenstraße, leads to the porch of the **cathedral**, **24** the **"Paradies"**. As the district of the cathedral was not subjected to the mundane dispensation of justice, the open entry hall served as a free place for all victims of persecution, they could not be prosecuted. As well as this, the poor people got food here and alms were given. Probably the porch got its name "Paradies" for this reason.

As the oldest church of Lübeck, its brickstone basilique foundation stone traces back to **Henry the Lion** in the year 1173.

Opening hours
April - September
10:00 am to 6:00 pm
October - March
10:00 am to 3:00 pm

Left side:

the triumph cross inside the cathedral comes from the workshop of Bernt Notke and is dated from 1477.
In the background the choir room for the bishops and for the head of the cathedral is divided by the "Lettner" created likewise by Bernt Notke.

The originally romanesque core was reconstructed to a hall church with a gothic east choir, later on decorated in a baroque manner. All of the three styles you find in the Dom are harmonically combined.

INSIDER-TIP

Directly beside the entrance of the cathedral, there is a collection of ethnology in the old custom house.

Art objects, things of daily use and religious cult objects from all over the world are collected here. The most famous exhibition object is the first mummy, that came to Germany from Egypt, bought by a pharmacist of Lübeck.

The legend says, that **Henry the Lion** erected the Dom at a source, which was worshipped by the heathens as being holy.

Opening hours
Museum of ethnology:
April - September
10:00 am to 5:00 pm
October - March
10:00 am to 4:00 pm
closed on Mondays.

With this he stopped the worshipping of the false gods in the town, which he had claimed for a bishop's seat.

As the source could not be completely buried, it found its way out and underwashed the fundament. That is the reason why both towers of the cathedral are not straight.

The cathedral by night

During the summer months there are guided tours in the cathedral late in the evening. Times and information: phone 0451/7 47 04.

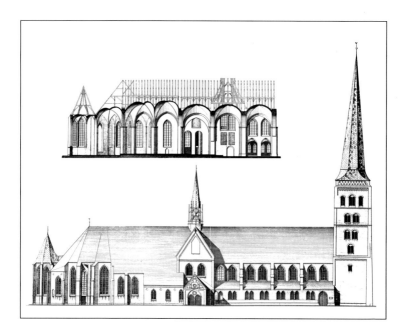

From the Cathedral and from the Zeughaus you go down the Hartengrube into the **Obertrave**. **25** Schwan's Hof, Hartengrube 18, is the **oldest existing alley-way** of Lübeck and got its name from the time around 1296 when the first accomodations were built by Johannes von Swane.

Nowadays many citizens in favor of an idyllic old town house willingly accept the threat of high water and the conditions being imposed on them by the preservation of historical monuments.

The narrow development of this site, extensive animal husbandry on smallest place and catastrophic hygienic conditions gave an ideal culture medium for the pathogen of the Plague.

Within a very short time the **epidemic anno 1350** killed off one quarter of the inhabitants of Lübeck.

For the growth of the town inside the walls new living areas had to be developed, as the river Trave prevented the expansion othe town as a

INSIDER-TIP

If you cross the pedestrian bridge at the Dankwartsgrube and look at the inner city island from the other side, you enjoy a special view of the fronts of the Obertrave with the Dom and St. Petri in the background. This singular perspective of the old part of the town gave the name "Painters' Corner" to this quarter.

natural boarder. In the back yards "Buden" (small cabins) were created with a space of about 20m².

During the summer you should catch a seat outside the **restaurants and street cafés** at the Obertrave. After lunch-time you can sit there in the sun, until it sets behind the Wallanlagen.

Along the Obertrave in the direction of the Holstentor and passing along the **music college** the road goes through the **Große Petersgrube** 26 up the hill of the old town center to **St. Petrikirche**. Stringed like pearls on a thread, the facades of the buildings in the Große Petersgrube 7-29 are architectural "pearls" of gothic, baroque and classic. The Große Petersgrube is the only street where you find completely preserved **original fronts** in a line.

In the building to your right resides the only music college of Schleswig-Holstein.

In the neighbourhood of the Kleine Petersgrube and Am Kolk the **Museum für Puppentheater** and the **Marionetten-theater** of Lübeck of Fritz Fey are situated.
The museum shows 5000 exhibits from all over the world, among them stages, requisites, barrel-organs, puppets and playing figures.

Puppet Theatre Museum
January - March
11:00 am to 5:00 pm
April - December
10:00 - 6.00 pm

The variety of the program ranges from classical plays and fairy tales up to varieté and operas.

The small alleys along the Kolk, like the Depenau, Marlesgrube, or Dankwarts-grube, invite you with roman-tic lantern lightening to stroll around or to stop off into the numerous **cafés and restaurants** of this quarter.

INSIDER-TIP
Marionettentheater Fritz Fey

Performances for children and adults in the Mario-nettentheater start at 3:00 pm and 7:30 pm. Every month there is a Matinée performance on Sundays at 11:00 am, no performance on Mondays.

Current program under phone 0451/7 00 60

Already mentioned in 1170 for the first time, the **wooden construction of the church** was replaced during the 13th century by a **construction of stones** with a three roomed romanesque church. Starting from 1250, the Plague caused havoc in Lübeck, lots of donations made it possible for two chapels to be additionally built in the 14th and 15th century. In that time **St. Petri** **27** got its basic form still seen today.

Opening hours
Main time Tuesday–Sunday
11:00 am to 4:00 pm during
exhibitions Tuesday–Sunday
11:00 am to 5:00 pm
closed on mondays.

As in St. Marien, St. Petri was destroyed by a bomb attack during the night of Palm Sunday in 1942. The first restoration works renewed the tower, the **lookout platform** and the roof, so that in 1961 the famous silhouette of Lübeck was completed with all its **seven towers**.

INSIDER-TIP

From the 50 m high platform of the St. Petri tower you have a wide view above the roofs of the old town island of Lübeck and of the country behind it.
Instead of stairs you have got an elevator inside the tower.

Changing exhibitions, musical performances, readings, symposiums to current subjects in terms of social policy today offer a program of art, culture, church and society.

Lookout platform:
March: 11:00 am to 5:00 pm
April - October
9:00 am to 7:00 pm
Dec. 9:00 am to 5:00 pm
Ask for latest times:
phone 0451/39 77 30.

Despite many architects working at St. Petri and despite new changes to the construction plans, a harmonic church room came into being with a reduced design which invites you to contemplate.

Personalities like Richard Wagner, Iwan Turgenjew, Fjodor Dostojeswki or the Mann family went to Travemünde for their summer holidays.

Travemünde was founded in 1187 by **Graf Adolf III zu Schauenburg**, and in 1329 Lübeck bought the village, in order to secure its power around the mouth of the river Trave and thereupon have free access to the harbour of Lübeck. Up to the 18th century, the economic base of Travemünde was the seafaring and the fishing industry.

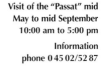

Visit of the "Passat" mid May to mid September 10:00 am to 5:00 pm

Information phone 0 45 02/52 87

More and more the small village became a lovely place for prosperous people of Lübeck, who spent their summer holidays here.

In 1802 Travemünde got the official title of a **Seebad** (seaside resort) and with this changed from a fisher village to a **health resort and tourist center**.

Already one year later the assembly room at the health resort opened its doors and offered the first administrations for one's health to the health resort visitors.

With the **ferry connections** to Riga, St. Petersburg and to Copenhagen, the health village achieved international status. The **casino** was one of the main attraction points especially for the rich people from Russia, there they met for the Roulette game. Lovingly restored, the „Four Seasons" Casino Hotel had been reopened in May 2003.

Having passed the casino and following the beach promenade your way leads you to the steep coast of the **"Brodtener Ufer"** (Brodtener Shore). Along a hiking trail above the shoreline you will reach Niendorf. We recommend this walk for bright days with a clear view.

The tradition of the annual Travemünder Woche makes clear that sailors and friends of the water sports always used to enjoy themselves.

Until today Travemünde is a popular meeting point for all sorts of water sports fans.

The landmark of Travemünde is the fourmaster **"Passat"**, which in 1959 found its last anchor place on the east shore of Travemünde. Instead of being scrapped, the ship is now under the protection of historical monuments and can be visited. In its windjammer life it rounded Kap Hoorn 39 times and the world twice.

In the Vorderreihe of Travemünde stilistically restored white house fronts remind you of the classical seaside health resort architecture of the 19th century.

During the summer season, on the opposite shore you can have a guided tour through the **oldest lighthouse** of the whole coast of the Baltic Ocean. You can visit this technical culture monument every Wednesday at 5:00 pm during the whole year.

Travemünde developed to one of the most important ferryports in the Baltic Sea area as well as the place to meet for yachtsmen and watersport fans.

EVENTS
AT LÜBECK AND TRAVEMÜNDE

MARCH

Lübecker Spring Market
At the Wallhalbinsel you find merry-go-rounds and stalls with lots of sweets for the whole family.

APRIL

Handel und Hanse
Consumer fair with exhibitors from trade, craftswork, industry and services at the Volksfestplatz.

Brahms Festival
The Music College Lübeck offers a variety of concert-highlights of world famous soloists and works of Brahms.

Kite Festival in Travemünde
The biggest kite festival in the sky above Travemünde with a multi-colored program.

MAY

Traditional Market anno dazumal
Nostalgic atmosphere of former times at the town hall market.

JUNE

Fair (Volks- und Erinnerungsfest)
The fair with merry-go-rounds and stalls begins with a big parade of the exhibitors through the city and lasts two weeks.

JULY

German Grand Prix Class 1 World Offshore Championship
German Race of Powerboats on the first weekend of July in the Bay of Lübeck in front of Travemünde.

Schleswig-Holstein Music Festival
Classical concerts with high-ranking musicians in the most beautiful places of Schleswig-Holstein with the opening concert in Lübeck. Annually changing themes.

Travemünde Week
For more than 100 years there have been sailing races in different classes, with merry atmosphere on the water, also for landlubbers.

Open Air Theatre
Start of the summer season for kids at the open air stage, where Pippi Longstockings meets Urmel of the Ice. Annually changing program.

Sand Sculpture Festival SANDWORLD in Travemünde
From July to August international sculptors form out impressive objects of a height of several meters and sceneries with the use of 8 mio kg of sand.

AUGUST

Duckstein Festival at the river Trave shore
Cabaret along the Music and Congress Hall with international flair, live music, comedians, street artists and pagodes with craftsmen.

Summer Opera
Classical performances at traditional places in the town and on the open air stage. Annually changing program.

AUGUST

Travemünder St. Lorenz Market
Around the St. Lorenz church place you meet people for celebrating, eating, drinking and trading.

Friendship Party in the harbour of Lübeck
There is dance and party in colorfully designed boats from 3:00 pm to 11:00 pm. The maritime loveparade continues in the clubs.

SEPTEMBER

Old town festival
Every second year on the second weekend in September the City of Lübeck is changed into a festival place. There is a party in the alley-ways and walks of Lübeck.

Harbour Party of Lübeck
The street An der Untertrave becomes a party road. At this side of the quai stalls attract people, on the other side of the water you can see the "ancient vessels of the ocean".

OCTOBER

Autumn Market of Lübeck
Equivalent of the spring market of Lübeck at the Wallhalbinsel.

Kite Festival in Travemünde
Colorful kites in the sky, colorful leaves on the floor: autumnly end of season in the health resort Travemünde. Kites of all different types of construction and steering dance in the wind.

NOVEMBER

Nordic Film Festival
Performance of Scandinavian, Finnish and Baltic films with an ensuing granting of awards. Additionally the most recent films of the Film forum Schlewig Holstein are shown.

TIME BEFORE CHRISTMAS – END OF NOV./DEC.

Craftsmen Market of Lübeck in St. Petri
Professional and hand-picked craftsmen show their works in the St. Petri Kirche.

Maritime Christmas Market in Warehouse no. 9.
Today the former harbour warehouse is a famous event place with a rustic-eccentric atmosphere.

Craftsworker's Market in the Heiligen-Geist-Hospital
Widely well-known and renowned market in a medieval ambience. With waiting time!

Christmas Market of Lübeck – Kohlmarkt, Koberg, Breite Straße
Festively decorated and enlighted inner city with popular hot wine stalls, sausages and pastries.

Fairy Tale Market
Between St. Marien and the Buddenbrookhaus the fairy tale market invites the little visitors to gape in astonishment and laughter. Small wooden stages show movable fairy tale figures, acoustic tapes tell the appropriate stories of the figures.

GENERAL INFORMATION

IMPORTANT TELEPHONE NUMBERS

To Germany: int. country code 0049,
Lübeck area code (0)451
Travemünde (0)4502
● *Police/emergency 110*
● *Fire department 112*

SERVICE-TELEPHONE

0 18 02/33 33
Monday to Friday 7:00 am - 8:00 pm;
Saturday 8:30 am - 2:00 pm

MEDICAL EMERGENCY

Parade 5, right side of the Marienkrankenhaus
Mo, Tu, Thu 7:00 pm – 7:00 am
Wednesday 1:00 pm to Thursday 7:00 am
Friday 7:00 pm to Monday 7:00 am
emergency telephone 7 10 81

VETERINARY EMERGENCY

Ask for vet on service: phone 7 10 81

DENTIST EMERGENCY

Ask for dentist on service: phone 69 19 13

POST OFFICE

(city center) Königstraße 44-46,
phone 70 21 50,
Monday to Friday 8:30 am - 6:30 pm;
Saturday 8:30 am - 1:00 pm

SHOPS

Monday to Friday 9:00 am to 7:00 pm
Saturday 9:00 am to 4:00 pm

BANKS

Money exchange in every bank
Monday to Friday 8:30 am - 6:00 pm,
Wednesday only to 1:00 pm

YOUTH HOSTELS/BACKPACKERS

● CVJM Lübeck e. V., Große Petersgrube 11,
  phone 7 19 20
● Rucksackhotel, Kanalstraße 70, phone 70 68 92
● Youth Hostel, old town center, Mengstraße 33,
  phone 702 03 99
● Youth Hostel Lübeck, Am Gertrudenkirchhof 4,
  phone 3 34 33

PRESS

● Lübecker Nachrichten (daily, except Mondays)
● Lübecker Wochenspiegel (Thursdays)
● Stadtmagazine, free
● Ultimo, Szene, Piste (monthly with events)

TAXIS

● Lübecker Funktaxen, phone 8 11 22
● Ossi-Taxi, phone 8 11 11
● Minicar, phone 7 10 11
● Maxicar, phone 7 44 44
● Radi´s Taxi Service, phone 4 42 44

IMPRINT

Copyright © 2003 by HVK GmbH

All statements were brought together with the best knowledge. Please help us with your proposals for improving, because as we know from our experience, you can never exclude an error. All rights reserved.
Any use of the text and of the photographs without permission of the publishing house is not allowed and punishable by law.
This work is protected by copyright.

Printed on **CREATOR SILK 135g/m²** three times silk matt painted without wood-free print with mediterranean white of **CLASSEN-PAPIER**.

ISBN 3-980-8982-0-2

Publishing House:
Hanseatischer Verlag Koller GmbH
Seelandstr. 14-16 · 23569 Lübeck
Telephone: 04 51 | 307 22 71
Telefax: 04 51 | 307 26 64

Photos: Thomas Radbruch

Translation: Claudia Vietze

Total Production:
SCHIPPLICK WINKLER Printmedien
Seelandstr. 14-16 · 23569 Lübeck
Telephone: 04 51 | 87 215-0
Telefax: 04 51 | 87 215-25
www.suw-medien.de